MW00511028

 Dogeagram: Understanding the Mystery of Dogs

(and occasional mocking of their humans)

Copyright

Dogeagram: Understanding the Mystery of Dogs
Copyright ©2019 by Jan Meyers Proett

All rights reserved. No part of this book may be used or reproduced in any
form or by any electronic or mechanical means, including information storage
and retrieval systems, without permission in writing from the publisher, except
by a reviewer who may quote brief passages in a review.

ISBN: 978-0-578-55333-7

Table of Contents

Canine Core Motivation

With Dogeagram, the important thing is **motivation** – to explore why a dog chooses to act in a certain way, and why.

It is this distinction that makes the Dogeagram fun to explore for we know that the deepest motivation for every type of dog is food,

with a secondary motivation for sleep and food,

and a tertiary motivation of playing fetch and food.

Then, of course, the concomitant payoff of love of the human, who gives food.

The Dogeagram is not to be confused with the well-known Myers-Dog Type Indicator (MDTI) or the Barkman Inventory or the DISC (Dog, Inside Dog, Social Dog, Car Lover). The Dogeagram is, in fact, an ancient well of wisdom that should be held in a sacred category far more than merely a human resource or psychological paradigm.

Praise for the Dogeagram: Understanding the Mystery of Dogs

"If you want to recognize the struggle and glory of the Dogeagram types, you can listen to my podcast "Dogology" in which I unpack all nine types in a way that is accessible and....very cool." – Ian Doggan Cron

"All dog types are actually just 'transitional types' meaning that all dogs try on their type on the way to ascending into their very best self. Dogeagram is a tremendous help in recognizing where the dog is in its transformation. We use Dogeagram all the time at our desert training center." – Richard Roverhr, The Center for Canine Action and Cat Contemplation

"The Dogeagram Creed changed the way we worship our dog." - Christopher L. Hartzcollar, author of "Sacred Dogeagram"

"Nothing has shaped my understanding of true core obedience motivation." - Don "Good Boy" Riso, author of "The Wisdom of the Dogeagam"

Overview of the Nine Dogeagram Types

Type One: The Rufformer

Led by the relentless inner canine critic, Ones live to make themselves and their pack better.

Strengths & Challenges | Ones have a "sense of mission" that leads them to want to improve their pack and home. They strive to overcome adversity and to live above the slovenly temptations seen in their drooling-and-always-pooping friends, so that disciplined canine glory can shine through. They tend to live for higher values (like making sure canines are revered above pygmy goats and cats and the strangely popular hedgehog) and making their humans proud. Healthy Reformers are easy-going and full of grace. Unhealthy Ones can be critical and stubborn dogs.

Type Two: The Obedient to Please

Twos are naturally intuitive to the needs of others and are empathetic and caring.

Strengths & Challenges | Relationships are everything for Twos. Their identities are built based on interactions with others – humans, dogs, butterflies, ants, birds, squirrels. Often caretakers, Healthy Twos know how to balance care for others with their own well-being, while unhealthy Twos care for others in order to feel good about themselves. Healthy Obedient to Please dogs live in balance and are loving, helpful, generous, and considerate. Cesar Milan can give a count on one hand of how many healthy Twos he has encountered. Those dogs certainly did not make it into a Dog Whisperer episode, because that would be boring.

Type Three: The Obedient to Impress

Threes long to be celebrated for success.

Strengths & Challenges | Threes long to be celebrated for their successes. The danger of this is that they can lose touch with their true selves and begin to believe their image. Which is imaginary. Imaginary cartoon dogs, and that's no fun.

These are the dogs at the dog park that everyone flocks around – both dogs and humans. They are the "class president" or "homecoming queen" in that they are the most well-rounded, attractive, athletic and intelligent of the bunch, as well as competitive. In other words - *you either love them or you hate them*.

Type Four: The Dog Like No Other

Dog Fours live for connection with their humans and relationship with other dogs, despite their belief that they don't belong in the pack.

Strengths & Challenges| Fours are in a relentless pursuit of authentic connection. Can a dog be an artist? Yes. At their best, Fours can help others to engage with their feelings through connection or artistry. Unhealthy Fours trust their emotions, but their feelings often tell them they are innately flawed. When this happens, Fours can become moody, unappeasable, and detached – and we all can imagine what it is like to live with a hormonal teenager who happens to need to be housetrained.

Type Five: The I'll Dig Deeper

The 'I'll Dig Deeper' Five dogs are private, self-reliant, and analytical. They study life and think about it hard before committing to almost anything. Anything. Anything.

Strengths & Challenges | Fives are the solitary, self-reliant, and analytical ogs. They can seem aloof, but they are actually alert; learning everything they an about the human, the room, the crowd, the scene, the field, the trail, the et's office. A Healthy Five brings curiosity and intellect, and an Unhealthy ive struggles to stay present (even if the command is, "Sit. Stay Present."). I'll Dig Deeper" Fives have a limited amount of energy reserves for much eyond their investigative exploits. Fives be lazy-ass dogs which may not be vrong.

Type Six: Of Course I'm Loyal, I'm a Dog

ixes are concerned with the common good. They are also deeply committed o loyalty. Because they are dogs.

trengths & Challenges | Don't believe the doggone lie that all are loyal in the vay Sixes are loyal! "Of Course I'm Loyal I'm a Dog" (OCILIAD)s are nique! Perhaps they should be called "Of Course I'm Loyal, I'm a Six!" ixes are sincere and engaged, but they also struggle with fear and resentment. f you step on the paw of another type, they will immediately dog-forgive you. o a Six, however, forgiveness is a sign of weakness, and they believe they nust guard and protect themselves from potentially hurtful humans and dogs, ats, cars, sirens, fireworks, vets, boarders, friends.

Type Seven: The Of Course I'm Enthusiastic, I'm a)og

evens are wonderful friends and companions. They are fun and optimistic, dventurous with a lighthearted spirit. Because they are dogs.

trengths & Challenges | Sevens make anyone smile. They are experts at onnecting with their inner puppy and they remind us how to play. Of Course I'm Enthusiastic, I'm a Dog" (OCIEIDs for short) are enthusiastic bout.... well, everything. Filled with curiosity, optimism, and a sense of dventure, they look at the world in wide-eyed, rapt anticipation of all the good nings they are about to experience. They have dogzpah! At their best, Sevens re bearers of hope. At their worst, they can be hardheaded, rarely following nrough on commands. They'll disobey with their tail wagging.

Type Eight: The Alpha-Alpha

Eights are action-oriented leaders of the pack. They love to take charge and always look for solutions. From forming a new pack, to conquering a new ope hunting range, to running a nice den, to scrap-yard dogging, to making peace -- they will lead the way.

Eights use their energy to "leave their mark" (which for any other type means peeing only, but for Eights it means literally staking claim to an arena of dogg life).

Strengths & Challenges | Eights find meaning in standing up for the underdog of the world (we couldn't wait to use that phrase – Underdog is a class act of a cartoon dog). At their best, they are supportive and playful, and engender trust. Unhealthy Eights can become aggressive and combative and are sometimes mistakenly typed as bullies. Eights fear being controlled and can be quite guarded.

Type Nine: The Family Glue

Nines are experts at adapting and relating to all other numbers.

Strengths & Challenges | If a dog was a chameleon, he or she would be a Nine (though also a very strange looking creature). Nine dogs are experts at adapting and relating to all the other types for the sake of peace. Nines know how to make everyone feel happy, but they can lose themselves in all the accommodation. They know how to validate the independence of others in the pack. These dogs tend toward roles in doggy diplomacy and have been known to take ambassador positions in the United Canine-nations (high level) or an at home-in-the-living-room diplomat (low level).

Now, let's explore each Dogeagram Type in-depth! Each chapter covers a different Type, so you, your dog and your whole pack can explore who it is that you brought home.

Before we continue, here is a note to:

All well-trained professionals who utilize the Enneagram

All well-trained professionals in the field of dog training

All well-trained professionals connected with the American Kennel Club, Westminster Kennel Club or the National Dog Show; all experts in canine breeds

What you are about to read is anecdotal, satirical, and in no way meant to be a comprehensive volume of research.

In other words,…. **It is time to lighten up**! *It's the Dogeagram.*

Chapter One: "The Rufformer"

The Rufformer: Dogeagram Type One

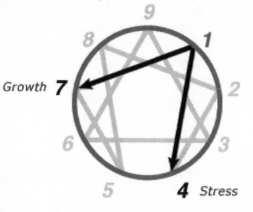

The Idealistic, Principled, Purposeful, Self-Controlled, and Perfectionistic Dog

Type One Overview

We have named personality type One The Rufformer because Ones have a "sense of mission" that leads them to want to improve their pack. They strive to overcome adversity and to live above the slovenly temptations seen in their drooling-and-always-pooping friends, so that disciplined canine glory can shine through. They tend to live for higher values (like making sure canines are revered above pygmy goats and cats and the strangely popular hedgehog) and making their humans proud. Rufformers like to hear a slight gasp when someone is assessing them. On the surface this can sound like arrogance or self-focus, but it flows from a deep desire to make other dogs and their humans proud; to make the den, pack and family a better place.

Have you ever had your dog give you the cold shoulder? Your dog is likely a One. They typically have problems with resentment. At their Best they are noble and can even display wisdom. At their worst they are aloof and seem almost put out that they must be a part of '*this family*.'

Rufformers are inspirational canine crusaders and advocates for change: always striving to improve things but are afraid of making a mistake. They are the uptight and self-righteous of the dog world. They try to maintain high standards but can slip into being critical and perfectionistic.

Basic Fear: being corrupt, bad or defective. This made for difficult research in that we could not find any dog let alone dog breed that fears being corrupt. In fact, throughout the genus Canis there is a strong propensity toward corruption almost to the point of being without a conscience, especially when it comes to clandestine meals, secret dug outs and bone thievery. We were confident that Standard Poodles would show a strong fear of being defective (in an aesthetic sense since they can't bear the thought of a hair out of place), but it turns out poodles just assume no defect exists ("I'm perfect!") therefore they are not afraid of it. Research also revealed that it is the poodles' *owners* who were obsessive about the dog's grooming, not the well-coiffed dog herself. Clearly some of the dark-side struggles in dogs stem from the dark side of their humans. I mean… *does this look like natural beauty to you?*

Basic Desire of all Ones: To be good, to have integrity, to be balanced. Ones are conscientious and ethical. Again, with the Dogeagram we think in terms of motivation, so ethics are in relationship to food. Rufformers have a strong sense of right and wrong.

It is right that all dogs eat, and eat good food, and do it politely. It wrong when dogs don't eat. It is also wrong when other dogs eat my food." - Saber, female German Shepherd One

Ones wish to be useful in the best sense of the word; they "have a mission" to fulfill in life. Some members of the working and herding group competitors at the National Dog Show display this, and it is often within these breeds that we find Rufformers. Akita, Anatolian Shepherd, Bernese Mountain Dog, Komondor, Portuguese Water Dog, Vizsla, Weimaraner, German Short-Hair Retrievers - - all hunting breeds, and herding dogs. Dignity, goodness and integrity in their mission make a One recognizable.

Fledgling Possible Ones

Enneagram One with a Nine-Wing: "The Idealist" An example would be Standard Poodles or Goldendoodles who tend toward the arrogant side but simultaneously get stressed if there is tension among the humans in the home.

1w9

Enneagram One with a Two-Wing: "The Advocate" Examples would be German Shepherd mixes, especially those with a Saint Bernard or Bernese Mountain Dog influence, or Siberian Huskies and Alaskan Malamutes who are quintessential sled dogs but enjoy doing the job with excellence and precision.

Shepherd/Labrador mix 1w2

Motivations: Ones want to be right, to be beyond criticism so as not to be ondemned by anyone. Remember, we are talking about the dogs here so try ot to consider your boss, teenage daughter or ex-spouse.

Vhen stressed, methodical Ones suddenly become moody and irrational at and nhealthy Four (the individualist 'Dog-Like-No-Other'). An example of this is helpful German Shepherd during a rescue – you'll see the dog thrive during le search. When the dog finds someone trapped, then the stress response of *this is not how it should be*" takes over and aggressive barking and distressed loans occur. However, when moving in their Direction of health, angry, ritical Grufformers (unhealthy Ones) become more spontaneous and joyful, ke healthy sevens (the 'Of Course I'm Enthusiastic I'm a Dog' type) – omething you'd see in on an open field when the shepherd can join more layful breeds in a pleasurable romp.
Ines have been known to leave their comfortable lives to do something xtraordinary because they felt that something higher was calling them. Rin 'in Tin and Lassie are examples - The idealism of each of these Ones has ispired millions.

Vhat is the motivation for being the lead, front dog? Is it a motivation toward eing the finest breed (One), is it sheer loyalty to the task and the owner ("Of 'ourse I'm Loyal, I'm a Dog" Six), or is it a desire to show off their speed and ower ("Obedient to Impress" Three)…? Only the sled dog knows for sure.

.laskan Malamutes can exhibit a One motivation, but only the dog knows vhat goes through its soul when the command, "*Mush!*" is called and the sled :am takes off onto the frigid tundra.

Malamute pondering his Type)

Ines hesitate and observe – they like to think things through. This dog will not respond unless the rationale for what they feel they must do is clear to them. This core motivation in doggy Ones is something way above Pavlov's paygrade. If they decide the decision makes sense in terms of their desire to make the world better - then they will comply. This is light-years from the general understanding of dog training stimulus-response.

Rufformers try not to give in to their instinctual drives too freely. The result is a dog who has problems with repression, resistance, and aggression. They are usually seen by others as highly self- controlled, even rigid. These dogs can 'hold it' on a road trip longer than most, not whimpering once to be let out to 'do their business.' This can be a nightmare for the human at the end of the road trip as they wait – and wait – and wait some more - while the dog struggles to finally poop his impacted-One-poop. Ones believe that being strict with themselves will make them the perfect dog. They aren't wrong. Except for road trip poop time.

Ones Relating to Others | You notice everything, and you're committed to inner and external perfection. You might want to read Brene Brown Dog's *The Gift of Canine Imperfection.* The phrase 'a good attempt at obedience' drives you crazy. Resist the urge to criticize yourself and other dogs and your humans. Practice letting things go. The sooner you embrace imperfection as a normal part of life, the sooner you can relax in the grass.

Relating to Ones | When relating to One dogs, it's essential to remind them that they are innately good. "*Good Dog! Good Boy! Good Girl!*" go a long way. Ones are also tidy characters, and they might be the only dog type who doesn't "snarf up" food falling from the kitchen counter – they will make sure everything gets cleaned up.

Chapter Two: "The Obedient to Please"

The Obedient to Please: Dogeagram Type Two

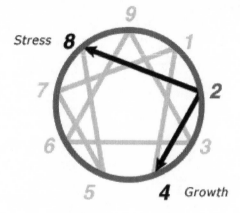

The Caring, Interpersonal Type: Generous, Demonstrative, People-Pleasing, and Possessive

Type Two Overview

Twos on the Dogeagram are empathetic, sincere, and warm-hearted (think Labrador and **Golden Retriever**). They are friendly, generous, and self-sacrificing, but can also be sentimental and people-pleasing (keep thinking Labrador and Golden Retriever). They are well-meaning and driven by a desire to be close to their human but can slip into doing things for others in order to be needed (you guessed it - Lab and Golden). They typically have problems with possessiveness and with acknowledging their own needs (though Labradors are born to tell you how hungry they are so who knows how that works). At their Best: unselfish and altruistic, they have unconditional love for their person.

Basic Fear: Being unwanted, unworthy of being loved.   Ingratiated obedience is easy with dogs who have not yet watched the Brene Brown Netflix series on shame. This is the shame-based group of doggies, but this can work in your favor.   Let's say your Golden Retriever is feeling insecure and starts to do the Golden 'nervous fidget.' You move carefully to reassure her until she relaxes and is indebted to you – it is at that moment you give the command to go upstairs to get your slippers. Shame can be a glorious thing when you leverage it!

Basic Desire: To feel loved. This is the Labrador Retriever. Always. There i not one single exception in the entire Labrador population. If you think you have a Lab who is not a Two….. well, we aren't sure how to help your misperception.

Enneagram Two with a One-Wing: **"Servant"** – Labs often 'serve' to get more love, and food (in unhealth). But Labs are surprising! They were bred to go into the Arctic ocean and the Maritimes in icy winter conditions to swim and retrieve birds all day, every day. They love to serve and will endure anything to please. Plus, webbed feet.
Enneagram Two with a Three-Wing: **"The Host/Hostess"** – If you have a dog who greets your guests at the door but does it with caution, discretion and quickly retreats to his/her doggy space, obediently staying there throughout the party – you have a healthy Two! These are rare occurrences and are generally only seen on episodes of The Dog Whisperer after Cesar has worked his magic.

Key Motivations: Two Dogs want to be loved, to express their feelings for others, to be needed and appreciated.   In other words, to be a Labrador Retriever.

When moving in an unhealthy direction, needy Twos suddenly become aggressive and dominating at Eight (Alpha-Alpha). This tendency is seen most in the sudden aggressive nature of a Two when moving toward a food bowel, bone, toy or rabbit. The aggression can be startling to one who is accustomed to the usual sweet disposition of the dog. The experience can leave shoulders dislocated (when owner is holding a leash and a rabbit appears), hardwood floors scratched irreparably (when the dog spies a chew toy under the couch) and other dogs traumatized (when the Two suddenly, voraciously lunges toward food). It is important to diligently protect fingers when feeding a Two snack.

However, when moving into health, prideful, self-deceptive Twos become more self-nurturing and emotionally aware. What this means is that the Labrador takes more time to snuggle by a fire alone or clean/self-groom rather than swoon endlessly when you are in the room. It is a mammoth relief *unless you are a narcissist.*

Twos are most interested in what they feel to be the "really, really good" things in life—love, snuggles, love, food, love, being pet, love, humans – especially children, and rabbits.

"*I cannot imagine being another type and I would not want to be another type. I like being a Golden Retriever. I like being one of the favorite breeds in Nort. America. like feeling compassionate, caring, nurturing. I like being the dog that children rush up to, instinctively knowing I'm just great. I like wagging more than barking. I wag when I know I have helped the person just by my presence. I can make my people happy, and that helps! I mean, seriously, why would you not want to wag all the time, even if you knock things off the coffee table*" – Madison, Golden Retriever

When Twos are healthy and in balance, they are loving, helpful, generous, and considerate (they make exceptional service dogs). But holy moly, their **shadow side is strong**: pride, self-deception, the tendency to become over-involved in the lives of others, and the tendency to manipulate others to get their own emotional needs met. If you have not experienced a Labrador follow you from room to room, you haven't experienced the dark-sided obsessive nature of a Two's need to help. And by 'help' we mean to love too much. When dealing with a dog in this state, we recommend the book "*Doggies who Love Too Much*" by Robin Dogwood or the classic Recovery Model materials such as "*The Language of Letting Go.*" Codependency is real in the soul of a Two Dog, so sometimes significant intervention is needed. The struggle is real.

Twos, along with Threes and Fours, are motivated from fear. All three types feel they must be or do something extraordinary in order to win love and acceptance from others. When this fear is allowed to rule, they may come off as generous and unselfish, but they have enormous expectations and unacknowledged emotional needs.

In the healthy range, the picture is completely different. Our own Yellow Labrador is an archetypal Two. Throughout her life she was found comforting someone in the family who was hurting, becoming a climb-on toy for toddlers and children, and forgoing her strong instinctive need to be close to me during a party in order to obediently stay on her bed in the corner. Again, this is a rare occurrence, but when you have a Two dog in a healthy state, it is time to raise a glass and maybe watch a few unhealthy two dog videos on You-Tube in order to better understand the special grace afforded you.

Personal Growth Recommendations for "Obedient to Please" Dogs

You will be less able to meet anyone else's needs in a balanced way if you have not taken a good nap in the shade, dug up your own bone for a treat and taken care of yourself properly (we're talking personal hygiene here).

Try to become more conscious of your own motives. Your type has a real danger of falling into unconscious codependent patterns and we promise you that you don't want to go to DogAnon meetings unless you like stale donuts.

While there are many things you might want to do for people, it is better to let your human ask you first. You must learn to respond to "No!" or "Off!" or "Stop it, Sweetheart!" (that last one means the human is super irritated).

Twos Relating to Others | You can find it difficult to express your own needs. You know the proverb about how we can't pour water out of an empty water bowl? Make it your goal to prioritize self-care and fill up that bowl! - it will help.

•   You will thrive in relationships when there is a mutual give and take. While it's easier for you to ignore your own wants and needs, this will only lead to Bitter Bone Syndrome.

Relating to Twos | The best way to love a Two is to help them love themselves. Make up self-care commands such as, "Sleep, you obsessive, crazy dog!"

•   Twos are also verbal processors, so being an excellent listener when they whimper and moan as you pet them will make them remember that being loved is as important as loving. Awww.

Chapter Three: "The Obedient to Impress"

The Obedient to Impress: Dogeagram Type Three

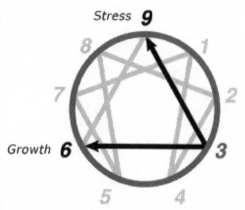

he Success-Oriented, Adaptable but Driven Dog Who Cares About nage

ype Three Overview

hrees are confident and attractive dogs. Full of life and ambition, they care out what you think of them, and are highly driven. They are very aware of e opinions of the humans and dogs around them. These are competitive dogs. was an "Obedient to Impress" dog who penned the canine best-seller *Your*

Best Dog Self Now. Other dogs are inspired by Threes, energized by them and not forced into a state of submission or intimidation. At their Best: Impressiv role models who inspire others.

We have named personality type Three The Obedient-to-Impress because when they are healthy, Threes really can and do achieve great things for the dog kingdom. They are often in the 'star' (achieving) breeds but can be an individual star of any breed. Their humans often look up to them because of their easy dispositions, great reputations and shelves full of trophies. These dogs also enjoy nudging other dogs to be more than what they thought they could be (much like a Rufformer). These are the dogs at the dog park that everyone flocks around – both dogs and humans. They are the "class president" or "homecoming queen" in that they are the most well-rounded, attractive, athletic and intelligent of the bunch. In other words - *you either lov them or you hate them.*

Threes are often successful and well- liked role models and paragons because of their good socialization, health and obedience. Threes know that they are worth the effort it takes to be the best.

Obedient to Impress Dogs want success, but only by how that is defined by their breed and their rank in the pack. In some packs, success means having a ton of socks, underwear, toilet paper and other stolen goods stocked away in some corner unknown to others in the family. Other packs value training, so success to them means scoring a blue ribbon at the regional agility competition. Success in other packs might mean practicing an escape route from a well-constructed fence. The Iditarod would be an example of an 'easy accomplishment' for sled-dogs Threes.

No matter how success is defined, Threes will try to become a *some-doggy.* They will not be a *"nobody no-doggy."*

To this end, Threes learn to perform in ways that will garner them praise and positive attention. As puppies, they learned to recognize the activities that were valued by their alpha or humans and put their energies into excelling in those activities. Threes also learned how to cultivate and develop whatever about them is attractive or potentially impressive.

"My mother seemed to nudge me to the top of the puppy pile from the very beginning," says Nora, an Afghan Hound. *"I was always the first out of the*

*uppy gate when it was time for our little bowls, and always consumed my
ɔod faster than anyone else. I think I was afraid that if I didn't, I wouldn't be
hosen. I was eight weeks old when I was adopted by my family; the pick of the
tter. I had no problem adjusting to my new environment. Sure, I missed my
iblings, but it wasn't anything like the horror stories I had heard in the puppy
ossip mill (so to speak). I was housebroken within a week and started
ɔarning basic commands at ten weeks. I always felt that I couldn't mess up.
ʻven with my insecurity, though, to this day something mystical happens to me
ɔhen I am in a competition."*

(They tell me I am hard act to follow!)

Basic Fear: failure and worthlessness
Basic Desire: to feel valuable and worthwhile

Ɔogeagram Three with a Two-Wing: "The Charmer"

Ʌeet our charming 3w2 **Jack Russell** terrier. Developed in England some 200

years ago to hunt foxes, the Jack Russell Terrier, also known as the Parson Russell Terrier, is a lively, independent, and clever little dog. He's charming and affectionate, but he can be a handful. He's as impressive as a charmer, and in his mischief.

Dogeagram Three with a Four Wing: "The Professional"
Think dignified Great Dane after a hard day at the office.

3w4

Every dog needs attention, encouragement and affirmation of their value in order to thrive, but Threes need them most. Threes want to succeed not so much for the accolades (like the Seven: "Of Course I'm Enthusiastic, I'm a Dog"), or for the feeling of superiority and independence that it will bring (like Eight "Alpha Alphas"). They want success because they fear that they are nobody and have no value. They excel in order to offset insecurity.

So here is the problem for Obedient to Impress dogs: in the intense pursuit to achieve whatever they believe will make them more valuable, Threes can become alienated from what truly interests them. Their quest takes them further away from their canine core. Have you ever seen a Saint Bernard excel in an agility course? Perhaps that's an extreme example on a breed level, but that is what it is like for a Three. Rather than searching for people lost in the wilderness (what a Saint Bernard enjoys), a Saint Bernard Three would put himself aside in order to perform even in a realm that is foreign to him. A more reasonable individual example would be a Shelty who appears to be a natural on the agility course, but who personally would prefer being at home with the new toddler in the house. This poor Shelty practices and performs every weekend, detached from her True Shelty Self.

From puppyhood, as Threes learn to receive attention from their humans and ursue what others value, they gradually lose touch with their desire; it is left ehind. If this tendency is not attended to, even the greatest Champion can ecome a shell of a dog. You can imagine a shell of a Shelty - - A Shelty Shell ells Shelty seashells by the seashore. Sad image, yes?

Examples of Potential Threes:

An "Obedient to Impress" type will likely be found within the **Weimaraner** reed. Weimaraners are so smart that they are sometimes referred to as '*the og with a human brain.*' Whether this is a compliment is dependent upon whose human brain they have, but for our purposes here we will assume it efers to humans who do not binge-watch *Breaking Bad*. Weimaraner puppies re born with striking pale blue eyes which fade to an ethereal amber to blue-rey as they mature, giving them a mystical quality that earns them the name Grey Ghost." Weimaraners have an exceptional sense of smell and can track nissing people (think homecoming king meets Good Samaritan award vinner).

Well-rounded qualities are good clues of a Three type, but it is the dog's nsecurity that is the revealing factor. In other words, if your dog doesn't now for sure that you love him or her if they aren't excelling, they might be a *Three. Or, you might be a jackass of an owner.*

A good example of this insecurity would be the Weimaraner in the movie *Best n Show*. The poor thing has neurotic issues that are the direct result of his naniacal owners who feign constant nurture of the dog when they live only for ne dog to be Best in Show. The pressure to be the best is just too much. This novie is for mature audiences, and probably not a movie for the humans to which we compare the Weimaraner brain.

Afghan Hounds are famous for their elegant beauty and have been since ancient times. The thick, silky, flowing coat that is the breed's crowning glory isn't just for show — it served as protection from the harsh climate in mountainous regions where Afghans originally earned their keep. Their huge paw-pads acted as shock absorbers on their homeland's punishing terrain. The Afghan Hound is a special breed for special people. A breed expert writes, "It's not the breed for all would-be dog owners, but where the dog and owner combination is right, no animal can equal the Afghan Hound as a pet."

Key Motivations: Want to be distinguished, to have attention, to be admired, and to impress.

When moving in the direction of unhealth, driven Threes suddenly become disengaged and apathetic at Nine: "The Family Glue." However, when moving in the direction of integration and health, vain, deceitful Threes become more cooperative and committed to others, like healthy Sixes: "Of Course I Am Loyal I Am a Dog."

Other breeds in which you are likely to find "Obedient to Impress" type Threes:
•   Jack Russell terrier. These happy chaps have high energy and can often give even larger dogs a run for their money.
•   Shetland sheepdog's trainability is truly impressive.
•   Standard poodle is known for its intelligence. And all doodles with poodle bloodlines display this intelligence as well.
•   Border collies are intelligent and energetic.
•   Australian shepherds are noteworthy athletes.
•   German shepherds are agile as well as intelligent and stately.
•   Any "Continental" European Hunting Dog

When an Obedient to Impress dog of any breed realizes the extent to which they have adapted their lives to the expectations of others, the question arises, *Well, then, what do I want besides food?*" They often simply do not know; it was not a question that had ever come up before. Threes heard the message loud and clear, "You are the BEST, Franklin!' – most dogs love hearing this, but a Three hears it and begins to live by it. The attention they received by performing may get them a ribbon, medal or even a sponsorship, but the dog never really knows who they are.

Here's where we all can have compassion on the Homecoming Kings and Queens - something we've likely never done before).

Personal Growth Recommendations for "Obedient to Impress" Dogs

Be truthful. Be honest with yourself and your people when you want to go out, poop, eat, play. Likewise, resist the temptation to impress others by strutting around the house. Gets old.

Develop a bond with another dog. Nothing spectacular is required—simply a few moments of quiet appreciation for the dog next door or your backmate. A Snoopy Greeting card goes a long way.

Take breaks. Curl up and rest! Don't feel guilty about loving your new ergonomic dog bed.

Get involved in a project that has nothing to do with your own gain.

Find a Rufformer friend and go to an SPCA meeting.

Threes Relating to Others | You are image-conscious and driven and prone to make obedience your goal. Remember, we love the real you. You are not what you do. Except when we need you to do it.
Engage with your feelings rather than burying them inside. Focus on the present moment rather than the future. Peace and rest come through Doggy Mindfulness.

Relating to Threes | The Threes in your life feel an urge to create a facade (a false dogsona) they believe you'll love. Vocalize your love for them as they are. For example, "That was an amazing hoop-through, Sasha! I know you love to do those." And then later in the afternoon, "You know that I think you are a wonderful doggy even if you didn't do the hoop-through just right. You are a beautiful Pomeranian just the way you are, even if you didn't score perfectly in agility this week"

Chapter Four: "The Dog Like No Other"

The Dog Like No Other: Dogeagram Type Four

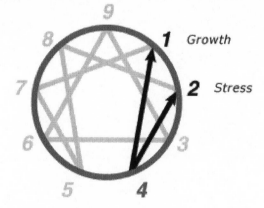

**The Sensitive and Expressive Type:
Dramatic, Self-Absorbed, and Temperamental**

Type Four Overview

To say that Fours are sensitive is like saying Mount Everest is a nice hill. They are self-aware and are comfortable with expression. They are unguarded and personal but can also be moody and self-conscious. At their best, Fours can help their humans to engage with their feelings. They are inspired and highly creative in order to create experiences so that everyone can feel, feel, feel.

Challenges come for Dogs Like No Other when they trust their emotions mainly because their feelings often tell them they are innately flawed. When this happens, Fours can become moody, unappeasable, and detached – and we all can imagine what it is like to live with a hormonal teenager who happens to need to be housetrained.

Fours feel vulnerable and defective, so they distance themselves from 'normal dogs.' They often display self-indulgence, and self-pity.

Basic Fear: That they have no identity or personal significance

Basic Desire: To figure out their significance

Strengths & Challenges | Fours live for connection and relationships, despite their belief that they don't belong. Even though Fours often believe they are too much and too complicated, they are relentless in the pursuit of authentic connection. Can a dog be an artist? Ask the humans who have a Dog Like No Other Four and they will tell you these dogs often gift their homes with surprising creativity.

Enneagram Four with a Three-Wing: "The Aristocrat"

The Greyhound is artful and dramatic in just about everything they do. These wonders reveal how form follows function. From the narrow, aerodynamic skull to the shock-absorbing pads of the feet, Greyhounds are perfectly

onstructed for high-speed pursuit. The lean beauty of the Greyhound has been n object of fascination for artists, poets, and kings and gambling addicts.

Inneagram Four with a Five-Wing: "The Bohemian"

Key Motivations: Fours tend to look for someone to 'rescue' them. This is not to be confused with being a Rescue Dog. Fours want to be rescued. Rescue Dogs have been rescued. If a Four was rescued as a Rescue Dog, they might be at a loss as to what to live for now that they have been rescued!

Fours need to express their individuality, cultivate beauty, maintain certain moods and feelings, withdraw to protect their self-image, attend to their emotions before any other thing.

When moving in their Direction of unhealth, aloof Fours suddenly become codependent and clinging as unhealthy "Obedient to Please" Twos. However, when moving toward growth or health overly emotional Fours become more objective and principled, like healthy "Rufformers."

Type Four Overview

We have named this type "The Dog Like No Other" because Fours feel they are different than everyone else – in every way. They might look exactly like all the other puppies in the litter, but as each puppy's personality emerges, Fours believe they are the most unique. Because of this, Fours feel that they will never be adequately loved or understood. So basically, if you try to love them - - *sorry pal*! Fours believe they possess special, one-of-a-kind gifts yet they also feel flawed. More than any other dogs, Dogs Like No Other are focused on their uniqueness and deficiencies. They are fascinating and exhausting.

Fours have low self-esteem and so they develop a Fantasy Doggy Self—an idealized self-image. Dogs Like No Other will spend time daydreaming about being a hero in a natural disaster, but never go to a Red Cross canine training. They will imagine for hours themselves as a therapy dog, but never put on a vest for training. A famous Beagle we know spends most of his time fantasizing about being a WWII flying ace. He doesn't realize there have been four other major wars since then, and he has forgotten to care for his human for ages. We would show you his photo but if we did, we would get arrested by Peanuts Worldwide, LLC (aka the Charles Shultz kingdom).

(A Beagle **in no way** associated with Snoopy)

In this way, Fours may try different identities on for size, but still feel unclear about who they really are because they base their discovery on their feelings.

When Fours look inside, they see a kaleidoscopic – looks nice, but it is overwhelming. Imagine the WWII Flying Ace in a blender with seven other famous dogs. Not a pretty sight. Very confusing. Pixar material.

Healthy Fours are honest: they don't try to hide or whitewash bad attitudes or behavior. They will confess to the Canine Priest or the Doggy Psychologist (aka Lucy from Peanuts). Healthy Fours are willing to reveal highly personal and potentially shameful things about themselves and can endure suffering. Fours must learn to let go of the past and not nurse wounds. I wonder what Lucy might say about that.

My doggy dating life has been a wreck. I have had a constant longing for whatever I cannot have. I am attached to the vision of the sweet Cocker Spaniel in The Lady and the Tramp. I took six different lady doggies out to scrounge for spaghetti, and not one of them was a winner in my eyes. Then I realized I was attached to the vision, not the actual female dog in front of me. Oops." – Buddy, Australian Shepherd

There is a Sufi story that relates to this about an old dog that had been badly abused and was near starvation. One day, the dog found a bone, carried it to a safe spot, and started gnawing away. The dog was so hungry that it chewed on the bone for a long time and got every bit of nourishment that it could out of it. After some time, a kind old man noticed the dog and its pathetic scrap and began quietly setting food out for it. But the poor hound was so attached to its bone that it refused to let go of it and soon starved to death." (*The Enneagram Institute)*

The story speaks for itself.

Finally, Fours are envious.
Dr. Gregory Berns, a leading neuroscientist in the field of canine cognition and author of How Dogs Love Us: A Neuroscientist and His Adopted Dog Decode the Canine Brain, tells of a 2014 study published in PLOS ONE which showed that dogs tended to display significantly more jealous behaviors (such as getting between their owner and an object) when their owners showed affection for a stuffed toy dog as opposed to a plastic jack of lantern. Seems understandable, right? The problem came from the Fours in the study – they started feeling wounded; threatened and envious of both the toy and the pumpkin. They became irrational and the researchers had to shut down the experiment. Fours make themselves miserable. Green-eyed monster, thy name

is Dog Like No Other.

Some examples of breeds in which Dogs Like No Other may be found:

Beagles. Beagle personality traits are loving, curious, and friendly. The Four type shows up in the deep howls that seem to come from the deepest emotiona well. Actually, more like hell.

Some Hunting Breeds. The emotional needs and intense energy of the Dog-Like-No-Other requires specific preparation for a prospective human. For example, if you are thinking of getting a **German Wired Hair Pointer** who happens to be a Four, it is probably best for you to begin your training by tending to your own soul. A lengthy spiritual retreat focused on centering prayer, grounding practices and breathing techniques will be useful, and likely the only way you will keep your sanity throughout the life of the dog. Anothei important part of your preparation would be to begin training for a marathon. Though training for local 10K is a good place to start, you need to think in terms of being a top performer in the Boston Marathon. This is another way o saying that relationships with Fours can be emotionally exhausting, and when the Four sensitivities are embodied in a hunting dog – it can be physically exhausting as well. Many bird dogs or hunting breeds can exhibit similar behavior. The Vizsla, for example, because of their Italian heritage, can be a Four in the morning hours but after a lengthy run (say…twenty miles at high speed) he or she can exhibit more "Of Course I'm Loyal I'm a Dog" Six motivations. By evening the full force Four moodiness and complexity will return, however, and the dog may begin an artistic pattern of some kind, whether it be a creative style of digging into the carpet, or a unique moan/how that, to the neighbors, sounds like some kind of intimate, personal activity they shouldn't be hearing.

Cavalier King Charles Spaniel

erhaps the most famous lapdog breed is the Cavalier King Charles Spaniel
ecause they are gentle and affectionate. These emotional and sensitive
ompanions live for spending time with their families and like to see their
wners happy, but they can be confused with their own identity and can get
istressed.

Australian Shepherd: The Australian Shepherd breed is one of the safest and
nost love-packed choices for all families who seek a new pooch. These little
ascals are very soft and loving dogs that are extremely emotionally sensitive
oward their owners. They are quite easy to train and work with because they
espond very well to whatever their owner wants from them. But if the false
mage they hold of their human or themselves gets jostled - - watch out for an
Australian Shepherd pity party. They only thing that helps them snap out of it
s a return to a day of herding livestock where they remember their True
ssence.

ours Relating to Others | This tension of wanting to stand out yet belong in
he pack leads you to believe there is something wrong with you, and therefore
ou envy. Remember that you are not too much, and it's okay to be
nisunderstood. It's also okay to have a small circle of doggy friends. Discover
eace by allowing yourself to be a dog – just a dog – just an ordinary dog.
Relating to Fours | Having a relationship with a Four can be overwhelming if
ou're not ready for the complexity of dog emotions but stick with it because
ours offer profound connection and joy.

ours prefer one-on-one interaction to group gatherings, and they need to be
old that they are understood. This can be surprising to a new owner of a Dog-
ike-No-Other when they take the dog to the dog park in anticipation of
oisterous play with other dogs. These folks are often disappointed to see that
fter a few perfunctory smells of a few foreign butts, their beloved Four is
nore content to wander in the woods by themselves or search out the smells
long the perimeter fence rather than joining in the rousing fetch fests of the

other dogs. This can provoke contemptuous rolling of the eyes from the Dog Park Pack – and by that we mean the *humans* who frequent the dog park to show off their dog's great skills amid other dogs. *Dog Park Pack Contempt Syndrome* is a true danger for the owners of Dogs-Like-No-Other because as much as we like to think we celebrate individualism, in the world of dogs there are like-no-other haters.

Be intentional to listen to Dogs-Like-No-Others because they need to know they are understood. It might seem that the dog is demanding the alpha role (understand me, don't ask me to submit), but it is just that a Dog-Like-No-Other needs coddling like no other. Trust us, giving them the assurance that they belong, feelings and all, will make your life more bearable.

Chapter Five: The "I'll Dig Deeper"

'll Dig Deeper: Dogeagram Type Five

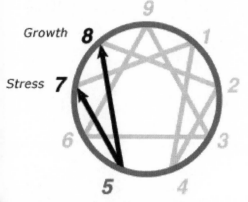

The Intense, Cerebral Type:
Perceptive, Innovative, Secretive, and Isolated

Fives are alert and curious. They can concentrate and bring their insight into developing complex ideas. I'll Dig Deepers are inventive, but they can also become preoccupied with their thoughts and imaginary constructs. They can become detached, high-strung and intense. At their Best: they are pioneers, forerunners; able to see the world in a way no one else has.

The Wolf: The Original Five
What was it, hundreds of thousands of years ago, that inspired the wolf to make the courageous and systematic decision to cross the windswept meadow and join the humans around the fire as they shared stories under the stars after

a hunt? The primitive and wild canine must have studied carefully, for more generations than we can know, the clues that led to the decision to literally change up the relationship canines had with another species.   The wolf must have seen that humans often had more food than they consumed, they appreciated loyalty, that they provided shelter and a sense of constant alpha energy to make them secure. It was data gathering at its finest, and then courageous movement that fundamentally changed the lifestyles of both species forever.   It is likely that not all wolves would have made this decision. It was a Five 'I'll Dig Deeper' wolf who courageously made the leap.

Or maybe it was just the food.

Basic Fear: Being useless, helpless, or incapable
Basic Desire: To be capable and competent
Enneagram Five with a Four-Wing: "The Iconoclast" – The Bassett Hound

5w4

The Basset Hound was originally bred to be a hunting dog. They are purposeful and systematic in the way they approach their task. They are prone to major health conditions such as Osteochondrosis Dissecans (OCD), gastric torsion, elbow dysplasia, thrombopathy, entropion, otitis externa, ectropion, glaucoma, von Willebrand's Disease, and canine hip dysplasia   So basically, they are iconic if they survive. Their loose skin also causes Bassets to have a sad look, which many people think adds to their charm (but is their Four wing showing up).

Dogeagram Five with a Six-Wing – "The Problem Solver": German Shepherd

5w6

German Shepherds happily serve as military dogs, seeing eye dogs, medical assistance dogs, and therapy dogs – all of which require innovation and intelligence. These qualities lend themselves this noble breed to being Ones, but you will find Fives within their ranks as they are consistently clever. They'll think through any problem and scare you with how crazy smart they are.

Key Motivations: I'll Dig Deeper dogs like to possess knowledge, to understand the environment, to have everything figured out as a way of defending against threats.

When moving in the direction of unhealth (stress), detached Fives suddenly become hyperactive and unfocused as unhealthy "Of Course I'm Enthusiastic I'm a Dog" Sevens. However, when moving in their Direction of Integration (growth/health), detached Fives become more self-confident and decisive, like healthy "Alpha Alpha" Eights.

Type Five Overview

We have named personality type Five The I-Dig-Deeper because, more than any other type, Fives want to find out why things are the way they are. They want to understand how the world works, whether it is the rocks at the bottom of a river, the way birds land on a field, the best path out of a forest, or the cleverest way to make their human laugh. They are always searching, asking questions, and delving into things in depth. They do not readily accept opinions – they must see for themselves.

"A day without digging is like a day without bones. Being a Five means always needing to watch, to take in the details of my surroundings, to be alert and study, to put my nose to the wind. This understanding makes me feel in charge and in control. I watch, consider and learn for a long time before I make a confident move." – Franklin the Doberman

Behind Fives' relentless pursuit of knowledge are deep insecurities about their ability to function successfully in the world. Fives feel that they can't function as well as others. But rather than engage directly to gain confidence, I'll Dig Deeper dogs hesitate by… digging deeper.

Fives spend a lot of time observing and contemplating—listening to the wind, watching an ant or spider, turning a bone over slowly with a paw. As they make observations, they gather data and gain a feeling of self-confidence. When they get verification of their observations it is a confirmation of their competency, and this fulfills their Basic Desire. *("You are a clever dog and we trust you.")*

In order to feel secure and confident, Fives need to have at least one area of expertise that allows them to feel capable. They will be the best scaler of fences, pursuer of deer or systematic disassembler of trash cans on the block. History is full of famous Fives who overturned accepted ways of understanding or doing things (Thomas 'Noble Breed' Jefferson, Darwin Dog, Einstein English Foxhound). Many more Fives, however, have become lost in the byzantine complexities of their own thought processes – digging, digging digging and never coming home.

The intense focus of Fives can thus lead to remarkable finds, but if they get fixated, it can also create self-defeating problems. This is because their focus of attention unwittingly serves to distract them from what's right in front of them.

Lagotto Romagnolo is a breed that comes from Italy. Its traditional function is a gundog, specifically a water retriever; however, it is often used to hunt for truffles. They display both healthy and unhealthy Five attributes.

(Classic Five Behavior)

Health

Dealing directly with physical matters can feel extremely daunting for Fives. Henry is a Bassett Hound who understands this:

"Since I was a puppy I have shied away from strenuous physical activity. I was never able to keep up with other dogs (have you ever seen a Bassett Hound run?). What's sad is that I started to avoid beautiful fields and trails, preferring to sit at home. I have always had a very active mental life, so I threw myself into mental and intellectual pursuits."

The problem for Fives is not interacting with others or increasing social skills. Henry has good advice for dogs like himself:

"Try this each day: become present and aware, see your personality in action, and don't act on your impulses. As a Five, observe your tendency is to be cynical. Breathe and relax until something shifts and your state changes—do you still feel the need to be cynical?"

The valedictorians of the dog world, herders took the top spot in intelligence rankings. You might want to explore with your herder dog whether they have considered being an I'll Dig Deeper.

The systematic intelligence of a Five can be found in Goldendoodles, Labradoodles, Whippapoos, Bernadoodles and Cockadoodledoos to name a few.

Oh, dear. Sorry, wrong species.

Here's who we mean:

Doodle Pup thinking about a lifetime of investigating)

Regular old poodles are the source of the Five brains behind the clever nature of all doodles.

Fives can be found in the smaller intelligent crowd as well. **Shelties** hold their own in herding, agility, and obedience trials partially due to their investigative nature.

(Sweet Five)

Then there's the littlest, surprising toy breed in which Fives can be found is the **Papillon**. They shine in competitive agility trials because of their forethought and intentionality. Papillon is French for "butterfly" and these lovely creatures will Dig Deeper than you might think.

Rottweilers likely descended from drover dogs in Ancient Rome, with a rugged, dependable disposition. An engaged Rottweiler owner will take care to

ain and exercise their pooch thoroughly because they need tremendous
ntellectual stimulation.

he Australian Cattle Dog is alert, curious and pleasant, the high-energy
erders do best with a job, and a job in which they get to think strategically.

ives Relating to Others | Relating to others is hard. You might wonder if
hey are worth it. You are brave for showing up when you'd rather be isolated.
elf-care is crucial. You can curl up in a corner on your own or take your own
weet time in the yard – let it re-energize you. Balance is the key.

Relating to Fives | Fives need space to process. They need clear and direct
ommands. They need encouragement. Fives will often revert to over-
hinking, so nudge them.

ives have limited energy, so dog parks are exhausting for them. They are
omfortable with stimulating routines (a consistent romp where the dog can be
ff leash and curious is great for them (although they dread repetition).

Chapter Six: The "Of Course I'm Loyal, I'm a Dog"

Of Course I'm Loyal, I'm a Dog: Dogeagram Type Six

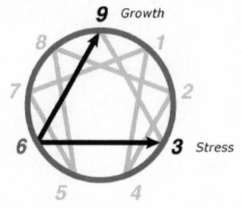

The Committed, Security Oriented Dog

<u>Type Six Overview</u>

The Of Course I'm Loyal I'm a Dog (OCILIAD)s are the committed, security-oriented type. On the surface, this type sounds like the healthiest of all dogs for Sixes are reliable, hard-working, responsible, and trustworthy. Press below the surface, though, and you'll find Six dogs can also become defensive, evasive, nd anxious—running distressed while yelping about it. They can be cautious nd indecisive, but also stubborn and reactive. At their Best: internally stable nd self-reliant, encouraging and leading the pack.

asic Fear: Of being without support and guidance

asic Desire: To have security and support

nneagram Six with a Five-Wing: "The Defender"

hough it is surprising for such little fellows, it is from within the **Chihuahua** reed weighing in at less than four pounds (the one above is about five ounces) nat the Six Types can be found. How can such a little creature defend, you sk? Their personalities vary, ranging from shy and timid to plucky and utgoing, but all Chihuahuas are fiercely loyal, and eat up as much attention as ney can get. They can also take you down if you threaten their human.

nneagram Six with a Seven-Wing: "The Buddy" Meet the Cairn Terrier!

No, wait - - that's a Norwich Terrier ("God loves a Terrier, yes He does!") - -

The Cairn's unique qualities, called "Cairnishness," include a short, wide head a shaggy and alert dog with eyes shining with intelligence.

Here's a **Cairn Terrier** 6w5!

A British breed club promotes Cairns as the *"best little pal in the world."*
Cairns are small enough for a lap-top snuggle and sturdy enough for a good
romp on the lawn. For humans who cherish the terrier quality of independent
thinking but true-blue loyalty, no other breed will do.

Key Motivations for Six: All dogs need security to be calm and submissive,
but "Of Course I'm Loyal, I'm a Dog!" types get this security through their
humans and reassurance from other dogs. They test the attitudes of others
toward them to fight against anxiety and insecurity.

When moving in their direction of unhealth (stress), dutiful Sixes suddenly
become competitive and arrogant at Three: "Obedient to Impress." However,
when moving in the direction of health (growth) fearful, pessimistic Sixes
become more relaxed and optimistic, like healthy "The Family Glue" Nines.

We have named personality type Six The "Of Course I'm Loyal, I'm a Dog"
because Sixes are the most bonded to their pack. They will "go down with the
hunt" and hang on to commitments longer than most. Sixes are also loyal to
ideas, systems, and beliefs—even to the belief that ideas should be challenged
(even Cesar Milan's ideas! Woah…). Indeed, their beliefs are sometimes

counter-cultural and rebellious.

The reason Sixes are so loyal to others is that they do not want to be abandoned. Thus, the central issue for type Six is a failure of self-confidence. Sixes don't believe they can handle life, and so they go to external support for guidance ("Take me to Dog Obedience Classes – the teacher will tell me how to live!"). If the dog obedience class ends, they'll find a mentor dog in the neighborhood. If the mentor dog moves away, they'll rely even more on you to train them, over and over. They may think and worry over the teachings. The OCILIAD Six dogs need the feel of solid and clear-cut instruction so they can become attached to their human. Then, and only then, can they move with confidence. Once Sixes feel they can trust their human, they go to great lengths to maintain connection with them, especially if the human puts up with their irrational behavior. They therefore do everything in their power to… stay loyal.

"As my anxious energy has become less, I don't have to check in with the Alpha-Alpha Eight before making my own decision on how loud to bark. I used to check in with at least five other dogs to see if I should approach the Alpha dog for her opinion! Man, I was a bundle of nerves. Now that I am moving toward integration and health, I can make up my own doggy mind." – Sandy, Springer Spaniel

Sixes, though, are dogs of contradiction. No matter what we say about OCILIADs, the opposite is often true as well. They are both strong and weak, fearful and courageous, trusting and distrusting, defenders and provokers, sweet and sour, aggressive and passive, bullies and weaklings, pack dogs and independent, submissive and dominant, kind and mean, republican and democrat. In fact, if you can't pin down your dog's type, they might just be an independent voter. The contradictions usually give this type away.

The biggest problem for Sixes is that they try to build safety in the environment without resolving their own emotional insecurities. When they learn to face their anxieties, however, Sixes understand that though there are dangers in the world, they can be courageous and have peace.

Australian Terriers, for example, are little dogs with grit. They are alert watchdogs and are quick studies when training. The desire to chase small, furry critters has never left them. Not always a great fit in multi-dog household because Aussies want you all to themselves. When they are peaceful, they are great examples of a healthy OCILIADs.

If the contingency crumbles, Sixes become anxious in their basic fear (*"I'm on my own! What am I going to do now?"*) A good question for Sixes might therefore be: "When will I know that I have enough dog food or stockpiles of bones?" If your dog is '**Resource Guarding,**' you might have a Six.

"Back off.")

You May Also Find a Six Within These Breeds:

Great Pyrenees

Like many herding dogs, the Great Pyrenees is a loyal guardian with a protective instinct. They're also calm, smart, and if you love vacuuming, they are committed to shedding. The Great Pyrenees is a flock-guarding breed; loyal to the flock, the farm, the land, and family members. Perhaps you saw the viral video of the Great Pyrenes who refused to leave his friend who had been hit by a car. Loyalty beyond belief.

The Springer Spaniel is also a likely breed for finding Six Loyalists. This fun-loving breed is "an enthusiastic worker" – loyal to the labor you give her.

Dachshunds. Though Dachshunds are small, they are very loyal to and protective of their pack. There are numerous stories about Dachshunds saving their families from house fires, and even bear attacks. Bred to hunt badgers in Germany, they retain their persistent, curious hunting nature, along with plenty of smarts. Dachshunds are known for their daring nature and will sometimes take on dogs or other animals much larger than they are – which is most animals except maybe mice, and chihuahuas.

(This guy is on your side)

Sixes Relating to Others | Practice trusting yourself first and cast-off skepticism. You have what you need to handle life, and some things are outside of your control. You don't have to conquer your fear; there will be food tomorrow. Be loyal for loyalty's sake.

Relating to Sixes | Don't tell your OCILIAD to not worry. Remind Sixes of your commitment and encourage them to trust their own experiences. Don't write them off as indecisive - - they just need time to think through their decisions.

Chapter Seven: The "Of Course I'm Enthusiastic, I'm a Dog"

Of Course I'm Enthusiastic, I'm a Dog: Dogeagram Type Seven

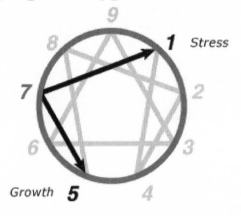

Does it all, all at once
Spontaneous, Curious, Optimistic, Scattered

Type Seven Overview

Basic Fear: Of being deprived and in pain
Basic Desire: To be satisfied and content—to have their needs fulfilled

Enneagram Seven with a Six-Wing: "The Entertainer" Why, a Corgi of

Course!

6w7

The **Corgi** is happy, smart, loyal, stubborn, and playful. They are cute little troublemakers who will make you laugh when they get into mischief. When they are given training, Corgis can certainly make everyone enthusiastic.

"Our Corgi Kandi is a full on 7 with a 6 wing. When she gets in trouble, she's like - Who? What? I don't know how that sock got into the backyard. Now come play with me! Don't you want to share that chicken you're making your lunch with?" - Shandi, Kandi's human

Enneagram Seven with an Eight-Wing: "The Realist"   You will often find 8w7OCIEIADs amongst Goldendoodles. They are a lot of fun, but when they enter a room you know it. They have the playfulness of Goldens and the arrogance of Poodles – a magical or toxic combination!

Key Motivations: Want to maintain their freedom, stay happy and not miss out. They have major FOMO (If unfamiliar with the term, see Facebook).

When moving in the direction of unhealth, scattered Sevens suddenly become perfectionistic and critical at "Rufformer" One. When moving in the direction of growth and health, gluttonous and scattered Sevens become more focused and observant, like healthy "I'll Dig Deeper" Fives.

We have named this personality type "Of Course I'm Enthusiastic, I'm a Dog"(OCIEID for short) because Sevens are enthusiastic about…. well, everything. Filled with curiosity, optimism, and a sense of adventure, they are like "dogs in the pet section of Costco" who look at the world with wide-eyed, rapt anticipation. They are bold and vivacious, approaching everything and everyone with cheerful determination.

They have dogzpah!

Sevens are anticipatory; they wisely look ahead. They also generate ideas "on the run" (ha - literally) which generates more things to do and plan. Their minds need stimulation. The classic game of 'hide the toy in the house while we blindfold you then ask you to find it' was created by an OCIEID who was bored and started initiating the game herself until her humans realized what she was doing. This is not just an urban myth – it happened in 1957 in Missouri.

Sevens are intelligent and well read – by audiobook from the back of the car, but still. Here is an example of an OCIEID's reading list:

> *"When the Doggy keeps the Score"* by Dr. Bessel Van der Mischief
> *"One Hundred Things to Do Before You Die"* – Dr. Jo Veterinarian
> *"Gravy Train"* – Melinda Purina and Sarah Iams
> *"Puppies Who Run with the Wolves"* – Dr. Canine Estes
> *"All the Beef We Can Not See"* – by various wholistic pet experts

They can be vocal. Let your imagination go with that one.

Their minds move rapidly from one idea to the next, making Sevens gifted at going from ball to stick to another ball to the trail and back to the stick. They take pleasure in being spontaneous so enjoy many balls thrown in different directions rather than one ball thrown in one monotonous motion over and over.

"I am definitely a stockpile-my-toys dog. It's not really for show or for memory's sake since I have a great memory. It's more so that my mind won't ruminate on where I put the toys if I put them in various places." – Goldendoodle Archer

"I was at a dog competition that was very hard to qualify for and was expensive for my humans. I couldn't sit through it. My mind was racing this way and that, thinking about my pack who needed me, a hole I had begun to dig but didn't finish; all the things I needed to do. Finally, I was so scattered the judges pulled me from the lineup. This was very upsetting for my human who took me home, put me in my crate alone and went out for a beer." – Frank the Corgi

Sevens have keen minds and are fast learners.t hey can be trained for agility, long summer hikes, Frizbee throws and swimming all in one summer – a true "Renaissance Pet."

Sevens struggle in this way: they feel they do not know how to make choices that will be beneficial to the pack. Sevens cope with this anxiety by keeping their minds occupied - for example by burying a bone, hiding a toy, checking on the children, guarding the garden from voles. This way they can keep negative feelings at bay.

*"I am a pretty productive pooch, but my mind has so many things to consider! I might guard the back door, check on the baby in the nursery, play with five-year-old Jack, nuzzle my lady human, and chew on a Nylabone – all in one morning! And yet, **I still haven't found what I'm looking for**."* – Bono the Beagle

Unable to decide whether he wants a knuckle bone, a biscuit or a bull stick, a Seven wants all three—just to be sure that he does not miss out on the "right" choice. While pursuing exciting experiences, the real object of their heart's desire (a T-bone steak for goodness sake) may be so deeply buried in his unconscious that he is never aware of how to find it.

Or, it could be buried in the yard.

On the positive side, Sevens are exuberant and upbeat. They have vitality and a desire to live in Carpe Diem! They don't take things too seriously. As we have seen, Sevens want to be satisfied, happy, and fulfilled - when they are healthy, they remind us of the pure pleasure of existence.

Breeds in Which it is Likely to Find Sevens:

Bernese Mountain Dogs. This sweet one originated as a farm dog, and perhaps because of this she is often a beloved companion who needs lots of stimulus. She has many good qualities, is affectionate and friendly, but heartbreakingly has a short lifespan.

Beagle: Though some Beagles are Fours, you can also find Sevens among their ranks. Not only are some Beagles excellent hunting dogs and loyal companions, they are also happy-go-lucky, funny, and oh so cute. They were bred to hunt in packs, so they enjoy company and are generally happy (except the moan from hell thing).

(Here I am again – still in no way claiming to be Snoopy).

Amongst Beagles you can find Fours as they fantasize about being a WWII Flying Ace, and you can also find the enthusiasm of the Seven's ever-present inner puppy. Snoopy would be proud.

(The Inner-Puppy of every **Portuguese Water Dog**)

From the beginning, potential little Enthusiasts Sevens maintain their puppy selves throughout their life.

Dalmatians. Dalmatians are family dogs. They are intelligent, playful, active, protective, gentle, social and non-aggressive. Best known as the star of Disney's 101 Dalmatians, this athletic breed can be coach, hunter, firehouse dog, and circus performer. Is there anything more Seven than a circus performer? The Sevens found within Dalmatians go from gallant to goofy to gallant again.

These two are not sure where the other 99 are, but they want to play. They also may be a little confused by current media conversations around the 99%, which they find to be too heavy of a concept for their playful selves.

"Am I a Seven or a Two?")

The Labrador is often a Two, but many Labs are Sevens. Labs' eyes glimmer with enthusiasm. Their "otter tail" seems to be forever showing eagerness. That is why, within Lab populations, you can also find "Of Course I'm Enthusiastic I'm a Dog" Sevens.

Sevens Relating to Others | You are sunshine in a cup, but your constant pursuit of more (more pleasure "Pet me! Pet me!" more food, more friends) can get wearisome. True peace will only come when you learn to balance this energy and embrace the present moment for what it is. Pay attention to who you're with and what you're doing. When hardship comes, "Sit! Stay!" The suffering won't kill you.

Relating to Sevens | Other types can show OCIEIAD Sevens how to hold varied emotions. Show them that humans are complicated with a vast array of feelings.

Be aware that your Seven's pain can manifest as anger or shame. They need time alone outside in the yard more than they know. Sevens can feel trapped by the needs and expectations of others. Such a shame since you'll be expecting something from them their whole doggy life.

Chapter Eight: The "Alpha Alpha"

The Alpha-Alpha: Dogeagram Type Eight

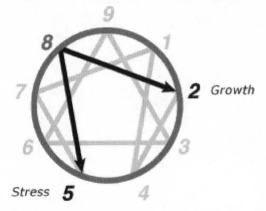

The Dominant Dog

Type Eight Overview

"When it comes to bull dogs, pit bulls, bull mastiffs – just give them more time than other breeds to submit." – Cesar Milan

Alpha-Alphas are self-confident, strong, and assertive. Notice we did not say calm and assertive. They are protective, straight-barking, and decisive, but can be domineering. Eights feel they must control in order to protect, sometimes becoming confrontational and intimidating. Eights typically have a problem dropping their guard and can have tempers. At their Best: Alpha-Alphas use their strength to make things better for their humans and other dogs and are magnanimous and courageous.

Basic Fear: Of being controlled by others
Basic Desire: To be in control of their own destiny so they can help others

Enneagram Eight with a Seven-Wing: "The Maverick"

The Chesapeake Bay Retriever is tough and tenacious, more protective and less welcoming to strangers than most sporting dogs, but with his family he's happy and completely loyal. Chessies like to be near their people, but they are independent.

Enneagram Eight with a Nine-Wing: "The Bear"

Good-natured and sociable, enthusiastic and bumptious, the **Old English Sheepdog** (OES, or "Sheepie") does best in the country, where he or she can peacefully tend to those around them (assuaging their Nine wing). Without companionship they become unhappy and destructive. A watchdog, not a guard dog.

Key Motivations of Alpha-Alphas: Want to be self-reliant, to prove their

trength and resist weakness, to be important in the dog world and to their
umans.

When moving in unhealth or stress, self-confident Eights suddenly become
ecretive and fearful at "I'll Dig Deeper" Five. However, when moving into
ealth or growth, lustful, controlling Eights become more open-hearted and
aring, like healthy "Obedient to Please" Two.

Matilda the Bull Mastiff

(Classic Eight)

We have named personality type Eight the Alpha-Alpha because, of all the
ypes, Eights enjoy taking on challenges and making opportunities for other
ogs. From forming a new pack, to conquering a new open hunting range, to
unning a nice den, to scrap-yard dogging, to making peace - - they will lead
he way.

Eights have enormous willpower and vitality, and they use this energy to
leave their mark" (which for any other type means peeing only, but for Eights
t means literally staking claim to an arena of doggy life). Alpha-Alphas do
his to keep from getting hurt. They know that protecting themselves requires
trength, will, persistence, and endurance—qualities they develop from
uppyhood.

Matilda is a Bull Mastiff who has struggled to understand her type Eight
ersonality. She recounts a puppyhood incident which has helped her make
ense of her defensive/aggressive ways:

*'Much of my toughness comes from my Sire daddy dog. He told me early on
o not 'let anybody push you around.' It was not okay to whine. I learned to
naster my weaker side even if I was in distress. We lived on a farm and at the
ender age of eight weeks a mean fox got into our pen and tormented all of us
uppies, growling, snarling and threatening us. I didn't make a sound and I*

stood resolutely until the fox backed down.   I could tell my papa was proud."

Alpha-Alphas do not want anyone to have power over them. They make sure that they retain and increase power. Power, man! Power to be the first in line on a trail, the first across the threshold of any room, the first to chow down at the bowls, the first to break a command but also the first to try to get a good nuzzle at night from their human.

An Eight may be a huge dog, little dog, mother of puppies, hunting companion. You can't recognize an Eight as easily as you think. No matter their form, they make an imprint; a mark. Again, we are not just talking about peeing and marking a territory – though they do that, too, proudly.

Eights are the true "rugged individualists" of the Dogeagram. More than any other type, they stand alone. They want to be independent, and resist being indebted to anyone. Although they are usually aware of what people think of them, they are "don't give a damn' dogs. They go about their intimidation, alone and confident.

Eights are tough and can take physical punishment without complaint—a double-edged sword because they could not care less if you do the "Shhhchcht sound while zapping them with your hand to realign their energy and get submission" thing.

Yet, they are so afraid of being hurt emotionally and will use their physical strength to protect their feelings. The 'tough guy' is soft on the inside. Alpha-Alphas get resentful easily. *"I would kill for this family. Why are they all scowling at me like that?"*
When Eights are emotionally healthy, however, they have a resourceful, "can-do" attitude as well as a steady inner drive. They take the initiative and make things happen with a great passion for life. Eights are authoritative—natural leaders who have a solid, commanding presence; when they are grounded, they are decisive and have good common sense. Healthy Alpha-Alphas use their power and force to create a better world for everyone in their lives.

Breeds in Which Eights are Found

As we mentioned, the Basset Hound can easily be a Five, but often their aggressive nature throws them squarely into the center of the Alpha-Alpha pool. This is especially true of male Bassets with other male dogs. Not to tereotype, but male on male Alpha-Alpha warfare through insecure and ontemptuous males is common among Eights. Basset Eights need a firm erson in charge of their feeding. *This is similar to why Congress has the ower of the purse.*

Here I am again, a firm defender of the patriarchy)

Doberman Pinschers. Healthy Eight Dobermans got their start in the late 9th century, when a German tax collector named Louis Dobermann wanted a nedium-sized pet to act as both a guard dog and companion. Translation: These fearless protectors can hold their own, loyally hang with kids, and be a riend of tax collectors. Kind of like Jesus, but a dog.

And then there is the American Pit Bull

Darn it, we keep mixing up species.

Here's what we mean:

t is true that the **American Pit Bull Terrier** has a bad reputation. But look at his fellow! In terms of motivation, when these strong and intimidating Alpha-Alphas let down their guard doggy-ness, they are actually very sensitive and verly emotional. This has been documented at least twelve times. Humans who love their Pit Bulls swear it is only their need to fight off other nimals that makes for an aggressive reputation. Hmmm. Perhaps the erception is real. They were bred to take down oxen. Have you ever seen an x?

Eights Relating to Others | You're a born leader, but sometimes even your umans feel bullied into following you. Remember that not everyone is action riented. Listen to commands! Include the human's wishes when making ecisions. State your opinions (we know you will), but make others feel seen nd heard. Peace is possible for you if you'll drop your guard dog persona.

Relating to Eights | Eights need you to at least attempt to match them. Honesty and straight commands are best (don't beat around the bush, specially if they are not in the bush). Remember that their aggression is not ersonal—they probably haven't thought about you in weeks. o have a healthy relationship with an Eight, be direct, and stay true to who ou are. While you can't force an Eight to have less Alpha-Alpha energy, you an help them think about ways they can help around the house. Oh, and one final thought. Alpha-Alpha owners sometimes get so accustomed o matching the energy of their dog in their commands that it becomes second ature to throw commands around. If you find yourself yelling, *"Leave it!"* vhen your **spouse** is picking up the remote, it might be time to take your eloved Eight to a doggy day care for a while so you can chill out.

Chapter Nine: "The Family Glue"

The Family Glue: Dogeagram Type Nine

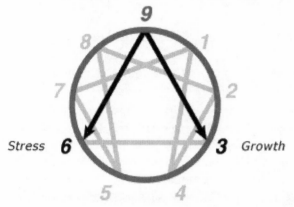

The Easygoing, Self-Effacing Type:
Receptive, Reassuring Agreeable, and Complacent

Type Nine Overview

Nines are embracing of all, and constant. They are optimistic and supportive but can also be too willing to go along with others to keep the peace. They want everything to go smoothly and be without conflict, so they simplify problems to minimize tension. They can be stubborn and lethargic. At their Best: Stalwart and accepting, they bring the whole pack together and heal conflicts.

Basic Fear: Separation anxiety
Basic Desire: To have doggy peace

Nine with a One-Wing: "The Dreamer": The Pug

9w7

Pugs are more serious, with a dry sense of humor so we hope they enjoy this book. The breed motto is "multum in parvo," meaning a lot in a little (or 'you might die from a canine disease,' depending) - plenty of dog in a small package. Pugs can be stubborn but even so want to keep the peace. They are affectionate; good companion dogs.

Enneagram Nine with an Eight-Wing: "The Referee": **The Boxer**

Boxers are sweet and playful dogs who were bred to take care of everyone around them. Their temperament reflects their breeding. They prefer to be in the company of their owners and are loyal pets that will fiercely guard their family and home against strangers.

Key Motivation for The Family Glue: resist disturbance or disruption

When moving in the direction of unhealth (stress), complacent Nines suddenly become anxious and worried at OCILIAD Six. Take a moment to envision a dog anxiously trying to keep other dogs in a pack happy. Not a pretty sight, is it?

When moving into health, self-neglecting Nines become more self-developing and full of vitality, like healthy "Obedient to Impress" Threes - this is surely preferable.

Type Nine Overview

We have called type Nine "The Family Glue" because no type is more committed to internal and external peace - for themselves, other pack members and all the humans in the home. They work hard to cultivate their peace of mind, and they also work hard for the peace of the canine kingdom. The thing is – "being woke" as a Nine can mean falling asleep to their true nature as they take care of everyone, champion every need for the family but their own.

Nines are either in touch with their strength or they are cut off from them, disengaged and remote. They either display the *"Weight of their Glory"* to use a Canine Stud (C.S.) Lewis phrase, or they are like vapor-like in substance. You'll know a Nine dog is in touch with her strength when she holds her head high and walks right past the other family members and jumps right into the back of the SUV, claiming her spot.

When out of touch with their strength, Family Glue dogs retreat into their emotional fantasies. When unhealthy dogs, Nines bottle up their energy until they are immobilized. When their energy is not used, it becomes stagnant. A sure sign of this is when your Nine dog is laying down on the carpet in the sun and they suddenly begin to 'run.' You think to yourself, "Awww... he's dreaming of rabbits" when suddenly you realize he is wide awake and just trying to figure out how he is ever going to stand up again.

We have sometimes called the Nine the holder of the Dogeagram as they hold the other types. The Family Glue can have the strength of Eights, the fun of Sevens, the loyalty Sixes, the investigative nature of Fives, the creativity of Fours, the accomplishment of Threes, the care of Twos, and the idealism of Ones. The only thing is missing is a strong sense of themselves. Being an individual dog who must assert herself against other dogs and predators is terrifying to Nines. They would rather defer or think about patches of grass and daisies.

"I am aware of focusing on the rest of my pack and what toys they might want. If I'm hungry but my person has a long day at work, I don't complain. I am realizing I might starve if I don't speak up about needing to be fed!" – Snowflake, the Newfoundland

The Family Glue is tempted to 'numb out' through any means (they have even been known to sniff the family glue!). Nines run from tension and try to find simple and painless solutions to their problems.

Focusing on peace is not all bad, of course, it is simply limiting. If Nines see only the happy outlook in every circumstance, reality gets skewed. As we've seen, other Dogeagram types have their distorting viewpoints, too. Dogs Like No Other focus on their woundedness and feelings, Rufformer Ones on what is wrong with how things are being done, etc. Nines, however, tend to focus on the "bright side of the den" so that their doggy bliss isn't interrupted. Nines need to recognize that all the other type dogs have perspectives that are true as well. Nines must resist the urge to escape into what we call "Nine Nirvana" which is their attempt at reaching a glimpse of the Rainbow Bridge long before it is their time; they want the bliss of the divine, far from the scary world.

Nines must remember that *"the only way out of the barbed wire is through the barbed wire, which includes a few trips to the veterinarian."*

Breeds within which Nines are likely:

Newfoundland

Perhaps the most recognizable Newfoundland is Nana, the canine nursemaid in Peter Pan. Nana exemplifies the breed's love of children and self-sacrificing ways. The Newfie is one of the great water dogs and when healthy she will display her power in the water, especially in a rescue.

The Newfoundland is a family companion but be prepared to put in plenty of effort training and socializing him, helping him find himself within the pack. The Newfoundland is calm, sweet and friendly, especially toward children, but he can be protective if the situation calls for it.

Bloodhounds: The bloodhound is a gentle, patient, noble and mild-mannered animal. She is especially good with children and tolerates too much from toddlers who climb over her. She also generally gets along well with other animals.

("Go ahead, climb on me. I should care, but I don't.")

English Bulldog: They have a sweet disposition, are dependable and excellent with children. The wrinkles on the English bulldog's face should be wiped by you regularly to prevent skin infections, because the Nines in this breed will neglect themselves!

("Skin problems? What skin problems? How are YOU?")

Saint Bernard

Saint Bernards are loving, gentle and tolerant. Don't let his size fool you. He is good with families and well-behaved children (do these exist?). Even though words such as massive, powerful, muscular and imposing are accurate, this is a genial giant. If you are lost in the wilderness, you want this sweet face to find you, not a mountain lion or an irritable forest service employee.

(*"You think I'm big? I'm only six months old!"*)

Relating to Nines | Try to include them in your decision-making processes and encourage them to voice their opinion. Give concrete choices rather than open-ended ones which can feel overwhelming. "Want to go to the Park?" is so much better than "Hey, let's go do something." If your Family Glue dog gives an affirmative bark or wag, praise them (and praise them and praise them) for expressing themselves.

Be watchful of your Nine's passive-aggressive nature. They tend to bury their rage and let it out in indirect ways. If you come home from a night out to find the trash all over the house, it is possible your Nine is trying to tell you something, albeit in a gross and unhealthy way. When they do bury their emotions, gently remind them that honesty can promote health, healing, and relationship. For example, if your puppy gets stung by a bee and goes into a corner to try to tend to its wound, coax it out so the whole family can express to the puppy that their hurts matter to them.

Nines Relating to Others | You love your family and you can see all the sides when there is tension. You are excellent at articulating everyone's feelings, so trust your bark, your presence, your nudges to communicate. You also see who is being left out - do this for yourself, too! Bark if you need to! Circle your tail! Whimper and Whine! Lean into the conflict and voice your doggy desires.

Credits:

Though clearly satirical and not based on anything more than anecdotal evidence, Dogeagram is loosely structured after the content found in the following books:
The Wisdom of the Enneagram, by Russ Hudson and Ross Riso
The Road Back to You, by Ian Morgan Cron
The Enneagram – A Christian Perspective, by Richard Rohr
Content from *The Enneagram Institute*

Photo Credits:
Best in Show: Castle Rock Entertainment
AKC.org
Newfoundland Photo: Dogtime
Vetstreet
Dog Bless You
Orvis
Pencil drawing of Papillon: Danguole Serstinskaja
Pencil drawing of German Shepherd: DJ Rogers
Pencil drawing of Labrador Puppy: Hulk vs. Abomination (Crema.com)
Pencil drawing of Peg: Hannah Asfour
Pencil sketch of Bloodhound: Getdrawing.com

About the Author

Jan Meyers Proett is a miner of stories, a crafter of words, and a lover of living things. She has been a professional counselor for almost three decades, which is why she needed this satirical outlet. Jan and her family have owned many dogs over thirty years, and she is appreciative of the Enneagram.

Heaven must go by favor. If it went by merit, you would stay out, but your dog would go in. – Mark Twain

Made in the USA
Columbia, SC
22 February 2022

56628204R00050